What's in this book

1 Learn about Chinese characters

2 Learn and practise

This book belongs to

_____

Learn about Chinese characters

汉字也可称作中文字。

汉字知多少

Past and present 过去与现在

1 Chinese characters have a long history. They gradually evolved from symbols that look like drawings to today's square-shaped characters. Look and compare the scripts below.

Oracle bone script, dated from 1300 BC, is believed to be the earliest form of Chinese writing.

Today, people in mainland China use these simplified Chinese characters.

甲骨文是刻在龟甲或兽骨上的文字。

2 Look at how Chinese characters have evolved. Can you guess what the four characters mean?

汉字从图画文字逐渐变得越来越方便书写。学生分小组，仔细观察第一列的甲骨文，讨论每个字表示的意思，再核对答案。

Past					Present	
⺊	⺅	⺇	人	人	人	(human)
⊖	⊝	日	日	日	日	(sun)
车	車	車	車	車	车	(vehicle)
鳥	鳥	鳥	鳥	鳥	鸟	(bird)

Today, the simplified Chinese characters are mainly used in mainland China. The traditional Chinese characters are used in some other countries and regions.

How were Chinese characters formed?
汉字是如何创造的？

The ancient Chinese mainly used four methods to create characters. Learn about the four categories of the Chinese characters.

很多抽象的概念没办法用象形字表达，于是中国古人又创造了指事字。

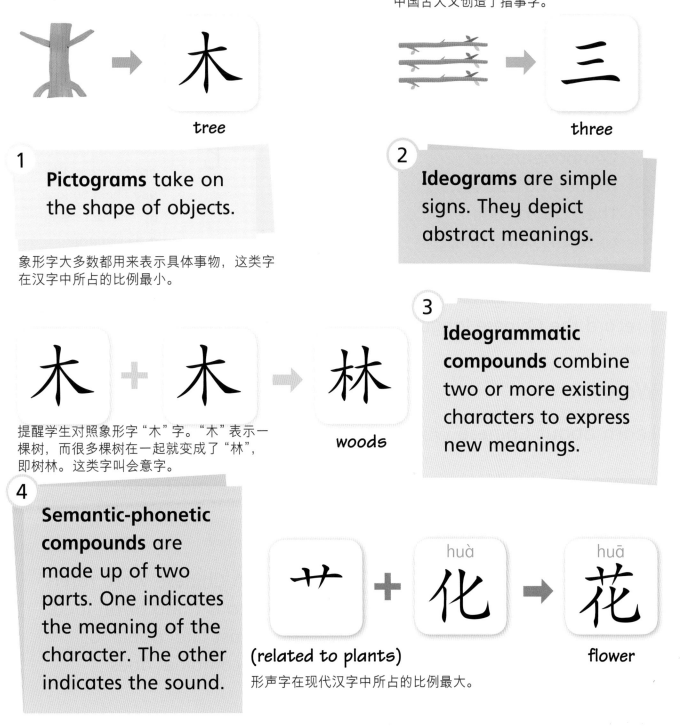

tree

three

1 **Pictograms** take on the shape of objects.

象形字大多数都用来表示具体事物，这类字在汉字中所占的比例最小。

2 **Ideograms** are simple signs. They depict abstract meanings.

3 **Ideogrammatic compounds** combine two or more existing characters to express new meanings.

woods

4 **Semantic-phonetic compounds** are made up of two parts. One indicates the meaning of the character. The other indicates the sound.

提醒学生对照象形字"木"字。"木"表示一棵树，而很多棵树在一起就变成了"林"，即树林。这类字叫会意字。

huà

huā

(related to plants)

flower

形声字在现代汉字中所占的比例最大。

Chinese characters 汉字

Strokes, components, radicals and characters

Learn about strokes, components, radicals and characters.

Strokes are uninterrupted dots and lines. They are the smallest units of a character.

Components are formed by strokes. They can combine to form characters.

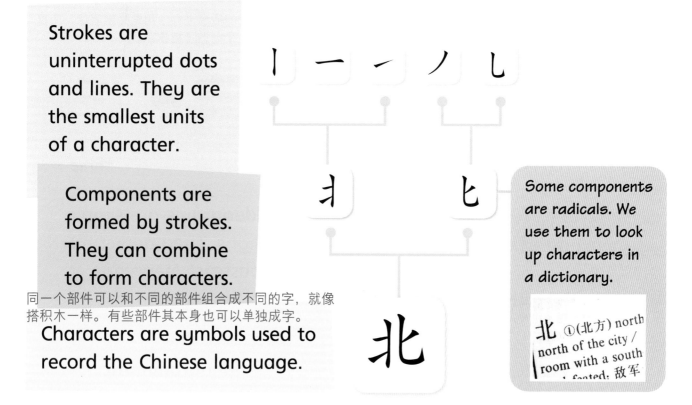

Some components are radicals. We use them to look up characters in a dictionary.

北 ①(北方) north
north of the city /
room with a south
footed: 敌军

同一个部件可以和不同的部件组合成不同的字，就像搭积木一样。有些部件其本身也可以单独成字。

Characters are symbols used to record the Chinese language.

Words

Learn about Chinese words.

Chinese words can be of one or more characters.

北
north

中国
China

A Chinese word refers to a thing or an idea, just like 'apple' or 'combine' does.

有些单个汉字表达了一个完整的意思，可以独立成词，另外一些则必须与其他汉字组合才能成词。

The structures of Chinese characters 汉字的结构

Chinese characters can be divided into whole characters and compound characters. Learn about them.

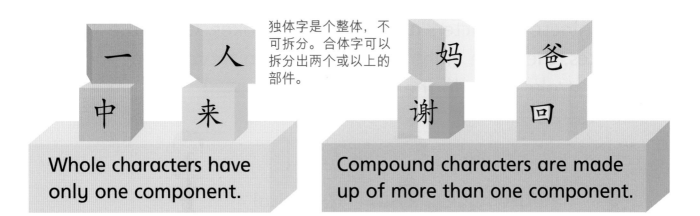

独体字是个整体，不可拆分。合体字可以拆分出两个或以上的部件。

一 人
中 来

Whole characters have only one component.

妈 爸
谢 回

Compound characters are made up of more than one component.

The structures of compound characters

Components can combine in different ways to form compound characters. Learn about the seven main structures of compound characters.

有些字的结构虽然一样，但它们相同结构部分的部件大小可能不同。如同为上下结构的"岁"和"爸"字，"岁"字上小下大，而"爸"字则上下差不多大小。

Description	Structure	Example
Left-right		好 妈 你 明
Top-bottom		岁 花 爸 笑
Left-middle-right		树 假 谢 游
Top-middle-bottom		黄 意 鼻 燕
Full-enclosure		回 因 园 圆
Semi-enclosure		问 凶 医 这 灰 可
Inlaid		巫 乖 爽 噩

2 Learn and practise 学学练练

Basic strokes 基本笔画

笔画是指书写汉字时不间断地一次连续写成的一个线条，它是汉字的最小构成单位。

1 All Chinese characters are built from strokes. Of all the strokes, there are eight basic ones. Learn these eight basic strokes and do the kung fu stances.

1 一 Horizontal 横

2 丨 Vertical 竖

3 丿 Slant 撇

4 丶 Dot 点

5 乀 Wave 捺

6 ⺀ Raise 提

7 亅 Hook 钩

8 乛 Turn 折

2 Which of the above strokes can you find in the pictures? Write the numbers and colour them.

做完练习后，老师可以让学生找一找教室里还有哪些隐藏的"笔画"。

2

7

3

5

4

1

6

8

3 Trace and write the basic strokes. 先找一找小鸟们的身体中隐藏了哪些笔画，然后再描写。

4 Trace the strokes to complete the characters. 让学生一边描写笔画，一边说说它们分别是第6页中的哪个基本笔画。

Stroke order 笔顺   笔顺是写汉字时笔画的先后顺序。

1 When writing Chinese characters, it is important to follow the correct stroke order. Learn the first four basic rules for writing characters.

1   From top to bottom

2   From left to right

3   Horizontal before crossing vertical

4   Slant before wave

2 Match the stroke order of the characters to the rules above. Write the numbers. 很多汉字的写法是以上规则的综合运用。

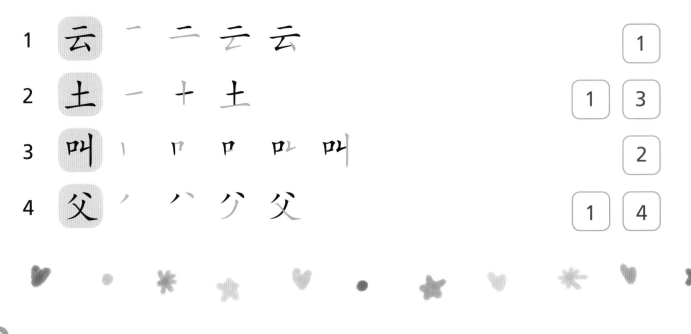

1   云   一 二 云 云   1

2   土   一 十 土   1   3

3   叫   丨 卩 口 叮 叫   2

4   父   丶 八 分 父   1   4

8

3 Learn the three remaining rules.

5 From the centre to the 'wings'   **6** Outside before inside

7 Outside before inside, but seal the bottom last

4 Match the stroke order of the characters to the rules above. Write the numbers.

1 日 丨 冂 月 日   7

2 问 丶 讠 门 问 问   6

3 水 亅 汀 汀 水   5

4 因 丨 冂 冂 因 因   7

5 Trace the character 永 in the correct stroke order to help the girl get home.

"永"字包括了汉字所有的基本笔画：点、横、竖、钩、提、折（弯）、撇、捺，也综合运用了笔顺的基本规则。让学生在描写过程中体会汉字之美。

Common Components 常用部件

部件由笔画构成，一个或一个以上部件可以构成汉字。

Look at the 50 commonly used components below. They are grouped under relevant topics. The ones in blue are also individual characters.

下方蓝色的部件可以独立成字。黑色的则是变形、调整以后的部件，现在一般不能独立成字。

Numbers

一
八 十
1 2 3 4 5 6 7 8 9

People

人（亻）女
子 父

Body

口 心（忄）
目 手（扌）
足（⻊）

Nature

日 月 水（氵）
火（灬）土 石
山 阝 田 雨
木 艹

Animals

牛 犬（犭）
鱼 马

Daily objects

米 贝 纟
金（钅）衣（衤）
门 宀 车
刀（刂）戈 工

Actions

彳 辶
言（讠）比

Adjectives

大 小
高

Others

口 又
寸 力

Numbers

1 Learn the components and look at the sample characters.

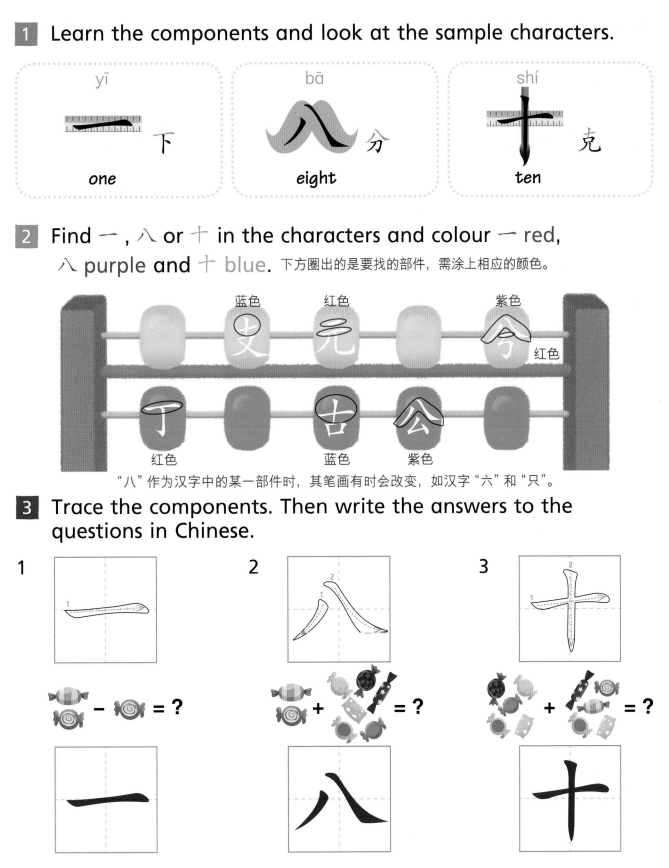

yī	bā	shí
一 下	八 分	十 克
one	eight	ten

2 Find 一, 八 or 十 in the characters and colour 一 red, 八 purple and 十 blue. 下方圈出的是要找的部件，需涂上相应的颜色。

蓝色　红色　紫色

支　元　勻
红色

丁　古　公

红色　蓝色　紫色

"八"作为汉字中的某一部件时，其笔画有时会改变，如汉字"六"和"只"。

3 Trace the components. Then write the answers to the questions in Chinese.

1

2

3

🍬 − 🍬 = ?

🍬 + 🍬 = ?

🍬 + 🍬 = ?

一

八

十

People

1 **Learn the components and look at the sample characters.**

了解各个部件的含义，有助于推测出含有该部件的汉字的含义。

rén

人　从

person

nǔ

女　妈

female

zǐ

子　孩

son, little child

fù

父　爸

father

2 **Trace the components on their own and in the characters.**

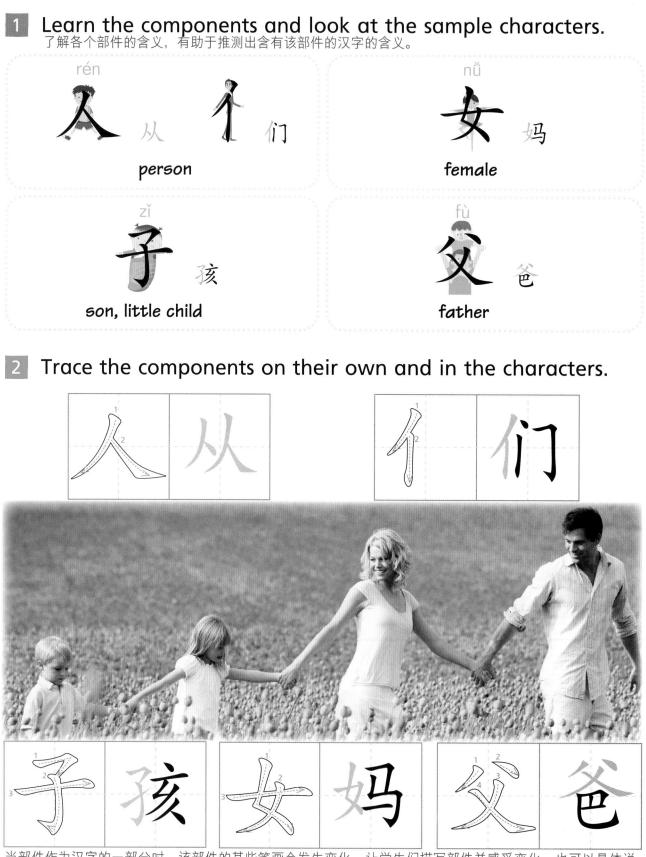

当部件作为汉字的一部分时，该部件的某些笔画会发生变化。让学生们描写部件并感受变化，也可以具体说说发生了什么变化。

Body

1 **Learn the components and look at the sample characters.**

让学生比较一下变化较大的几个部件，并具体说说。

kǒu

口 叫

mouth

xīn

心 想 忄 情

heart

mù

目 眼

eye

shǒu

手 拿 扌 打

hand

zú

足 捉 ⻊ 跑

foot

2 **Trace and write the components.**

描写部件的同时，观察图片中相应的
位置，更好地理解部件所表达的意思。

Nature

1 Learn the components and look at the sample characters.

下面的部件跟事物本身的形态很相像。

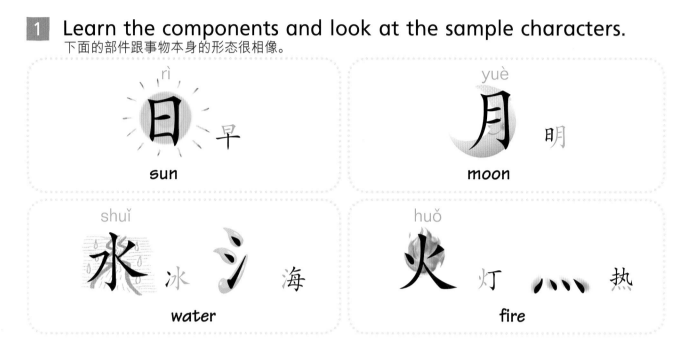

rì
日 早
sun

yuè
月 明
moon

shuǐ
水 冰 氵 海
water

huǒ
火 灯 灬 热
fire

2 Trace and write the components. Then colour 日 , 月 , 水 and 火 in the pictures using the corresponding colours.

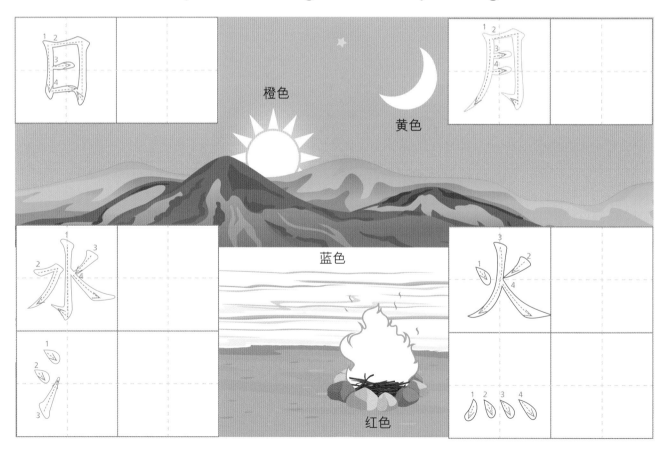

橙色

黄色

蓝色

红色

3 Learn the components and look at the sample characters.

下面的部件跟事物本身的形态很相像。

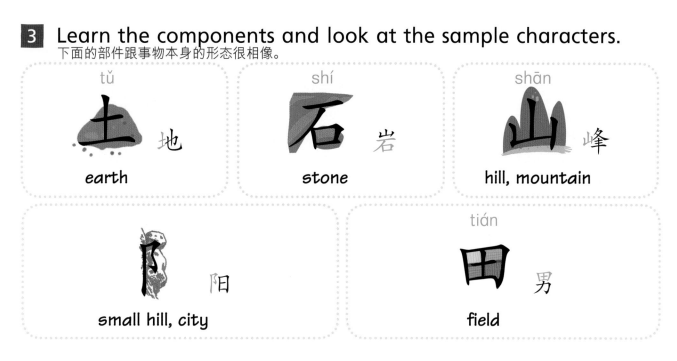

tǔ	shí	shān
土 地	石 岩	山 峰
earth	stone	hill, mountain

阝 阳	田 男
small hill, city	field
tián	

4 Trace the components and colour them in the characters using the corresponding colours. 下方圈出的是要找的部件，需涂上相应的颜色。

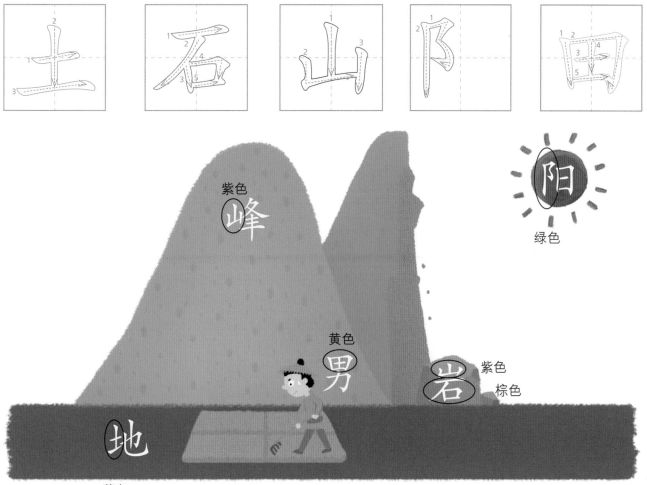

紫色 峰

绿色 阳

黄色 男

紫色 棕色 岩

蓝色 地

5 Learn the components and look at the sample characters.

下面的部件跟事物本身的形态很相像。

yǔ

雨 雪

rain

mù

木 林

tree, wood

⺿ 草

grass

6 Which characters have 雨 , 木 or ⺿ in them? Colour
these boxes. What number can you see? 37

圈中的汉字含有要找的
部件，需要涂色。

蓝	机	雾	很	草	雪	苗
饭	球	霉	耳	笔	衫	森
树	林	菜	看	铅	茶	电
海	地	橡	黑	快	板	宝
花	霞	雷	画	晚	零	帽

7 Trace the components on their own and in the characters.

描写完后，可以说说为什么
这些字用了相应的部件，想
表达什么含义。

Animals

1 **Learn the components and look at the sample characters.**

了解各个部件的含义，有助于推测出含有该部件的汉字的含义。

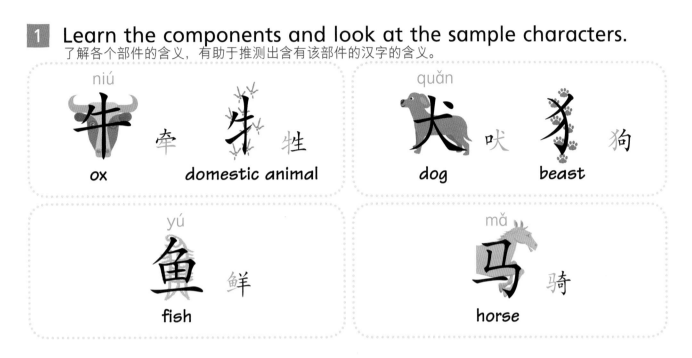

niú
牛 牵
ox domestic animal

quǎn
犬 吠 狗
dog beast

yú
鱼 鲜
fish

mǎ
马 骑
horse

2 **Trace the components on their own and in the characters.**

可以先想想这些图片各表达了什么意思，然后再描写相应的汉字。

Daily objects

1 Learn the components and look at the sample characters.

了解各个部件的含义，有助于推测出含有该部件的汉字的含义。

mǐ	bèi	
米 粒	贝 财	纟 线
rice	shell	silk, thread

jīn	yī
金 鉴 钅 钱	衣 裳 衤 裤
gold	clothes

2 Trace the components on their own and in the characters.

观察图片，并描写部件，体会部件的意思。

3 Learn the components and look at the sample characters.
了解各个部件的含义，有助于推测出含有该部件的汉字的含义。

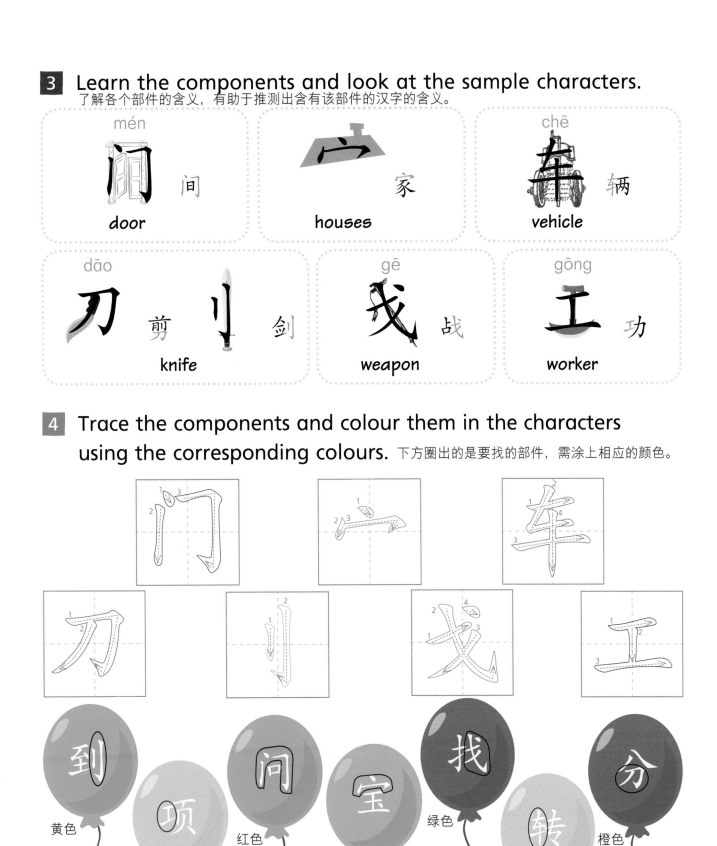

mén
门
门 door

chē
车
辆 vehicle

家 houses

dāo
刀 刂
剪 剑 knife

gē
戈
战 weapon

gōng
工
功 worker

4 Trace the components and colour them in the characters using the corresponding colours. 下方圈出的是要找的部件，需涂上相应的颜色。

到 黄色
项 粉色
问 红色
宝 蓝色
找 绿色
转 紫色
分 橙色

Actions

1 **Learn the components and look at the sample characters.**

了解各个部件的含义，有助于推测出含有该部件的汉字的含义。

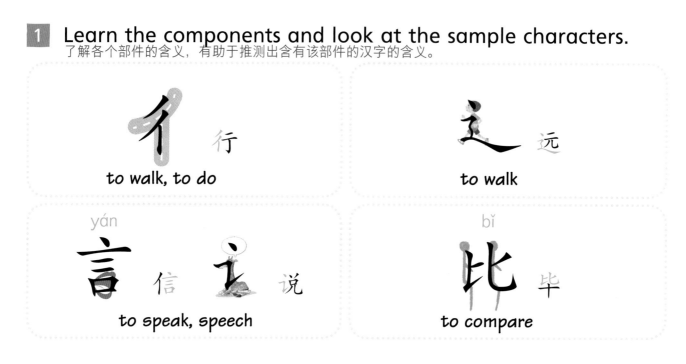

行
to walk, to do

远
to walk

yán
言　信　说
to speak, speech

bǐ
比　毕
to compare

2 **Trace and write the components. Which characters on the biscuits have these components in them? Match them to the components.**

完成连线后，观察未连线的汉字的部件，然后说说它们与本页的哪些部件很相似，又有什么区别。

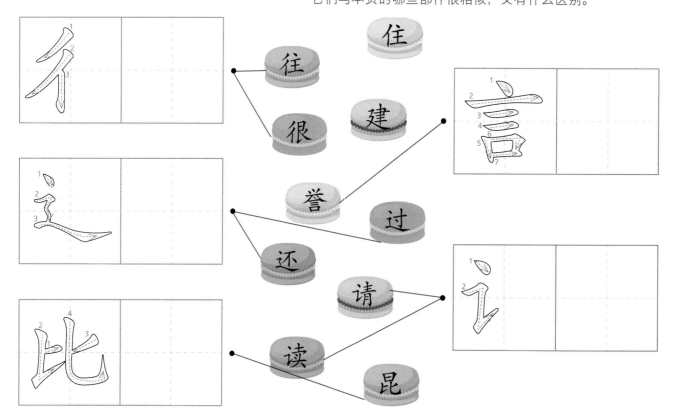

Adjectives

1 Learn the components and look at the sample characters.

dà	xiǎo	gāo
大 尖	小 孙	高 搞
big	**small**	**tall**

2 Trace and write the components. Then colour the balls with the component 大 red, the ones with 小 yellow and the others with 高 blue.

Others

1 Learn the components and look at the sample characters.

提醒学生国字框与"口"不同；并让学生区分"寸"和"十"、"力"和"刀"的不同。

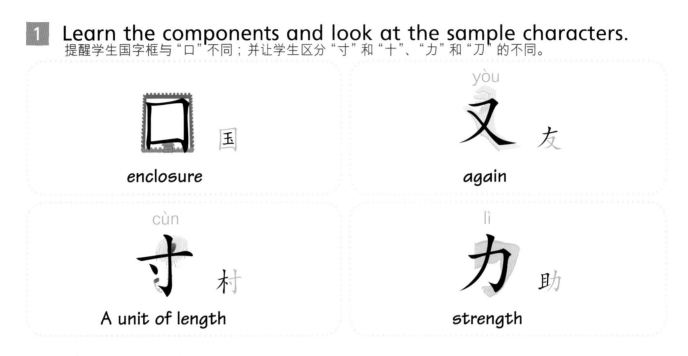

口 玉
enclosure

yòu
又 友
again

cùn
寸 村
A unit of length

lì
力 助
strength

2 Trace and write the components. Which characters have these components in them? Circle the correct ones.

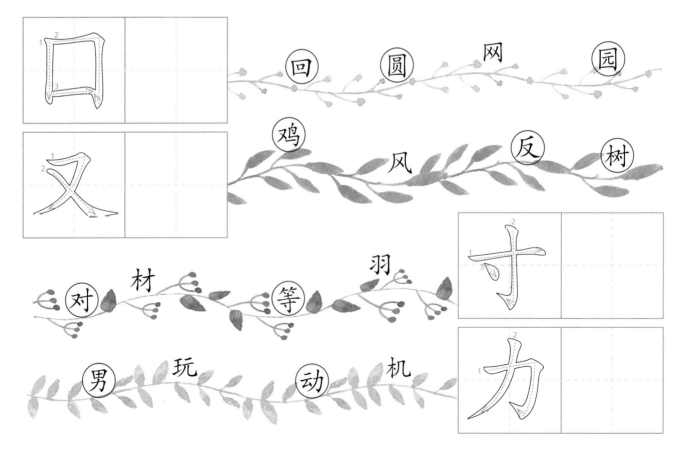

口

又

回　圆　网　园

鸡　风　反　树

寸

力

对　材　等　羽

男　玩　动　机

Revision 复习

1 Look carefully. Write the letters.

老师可以多准备一些学生已学的汉字拆开后的笔画，让学生自己组成部件，最后组成汉字，并大致说说这个汉字的意思。

a Components
b Character
c Strokes

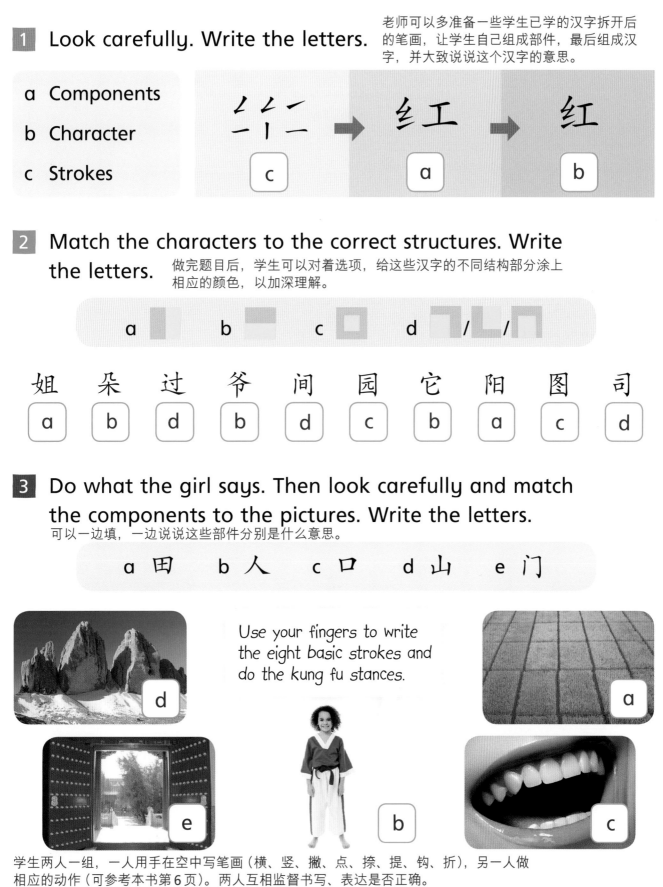

丿丨一 → 纟工 → 红

c   a   b

2 Match the characters to the correct structures. Write the letters.

做完题目后，学生可以对着选项，给这些汉字的不同结构部分涂上相应的颜色，以加深理解。

a ▮ b ▬ c ▢ d ⅂/乚/凵

姐 朵 过 爷 间 园 它 阳 图 司
a   b   d   b   d   c   b   a   c   d

3 Do what the girl says. Then look carefully and match the components to the pictures. Write the letters.

可以一边填，一边说说这些部件分别是什么意思。

a 田   b 人   c 口   d 山   e 门

Use your fingers to write the eight basic strokes and do the kung fu stances.

学生两人一组，一人用手在空中写笔画（横、竖、撇、点、捺、提、钩、折），另一人做相应的动作（可参考本书第6页）。两人互相监督书写、表达是否正确。

OXFORD
UNIVERSITY PRESS

Oxford University Press is a department of the University of Oxford.
It furthers the University's objective of excellence in research, scholarship,
and education by publishing worldwide. Oxford is a registered trade mark of
Oxford University Press in the UK and in certain other countries

Published in Hong Kong by
Oxford University Press (China) Limited
39th Floor, One Kowloon, 1 Wang Yuen Street, Kowloon Bay,
Hong Kong

Illustrated by Emily Chan

Photographs for reproduction permitted by Dreamstime.com

China National Publications Import & Export (Group) Corporation is an authorized distributor of
Oxford Elementary Chinese.

Please contact content@cnpiec.com.cn or 86-10-65856782

ISBN: 978-0-19-082364-1

10 9 8 7 6 5 4 3

Teacher's Edition
ISBN: 978-0-19-082367-2

10 9 8 7 6 5 4 3 2